# AUTHOR BIOGRAPHY

Robert Halliday was born in Cambridge, but moved to Bury St. Edmunds with his family in 1966, attending Tollgate Primary School, King Edward VI School and the West Suffolk College in the town. He began exploring historic churches at the age of ten: this interest initially prompted him to investigate gravestones. Holding B.A. and M.A. degrees in history from North London Polytechnic and the State University of New York at Binghamton in the U.S.A., he spends his spare time researching unusual aspects of history and folklore. He is the author of *Cambridge Ghosts* (co-written with Alan Murdie, and also published by Arima Publishing), *Cambridgeshire Strange But True*, *Suffolk Strange But True* and *Around Bury St. Edmunds in Old Photographs*, as well as articles in popular and academic journals. His other interests include eyebath collecting (he owns over 150 different specimens). He has recently taken up horseriding.

Suffolk
Graves

# A HISTORY OF
# SUFFOLK GRAVESTONES

Robert Halliday

*Robert Halliday*

Published 2013 by arima publishing

www.arimapublishing.com

ISBN 978 1 84549 595 4

© 2013 Robert Halliday

Printed and bound in the United Kingdom

Typeset in Garamond

arima publishing
ASK House, Northgate Avenue
Bury St Edmunds, Suffolk IP32 6BB
t: (+44) 01284 700321
www.arimapublishing.com

To
Jonathan Green
in appreciation of his friendship
over many years.

# CONTENTS

# INTRODUCTION

Although I began exploring historic churches in the mid-1960s, when was about ten, it was only in 2003 that I realised the importance and significance of gravestones and churchyard memorials. While churches are centres of religious observance, they also commemorate and honour past generations. The churchyard is a sacred area, containing the remains of those who have shared in the life of the church or the community. Churchyard memorials are thus an essential and integral part of the church. They can tell us about the people who were associated with the church, and contributed to the community or the wider world, and how people, or those who knew them, wanted to be remembered. This prompted me to make an investigation of the churchyard (and cemetery) memorials in Suffolk, to see how they originated, and how they have developed over the centuries. It is hoped that this book will help to further the realisation that, if historic (and modern) churches are worth visiting, it is also rewarding to explore the surrounding churchyards and to study and appreciate the gravestones and churchyard memorials that might be seen there.

Churchyard monuments are a visible link with past generations. Recalling those who contributed to the church, the community, or the wider world, they can also be of great historic and artistic interest. Their origins are linked with the development of Christian burial practice, particularly in East Anglia. Christianity entered Britain under the Roman Empire, and was accepted by most of the Romano-British population after 313, when it became the official religion of the Empire. In 1974 Stanley West, the county archaeologist for Suffolk, directed an excavation at Icklingham which uncovered the foundations of a fourth century church, incorporating a 'baptistry', a chamber where people were christened. Nearby the excavators found a circular lead font, embellished with Christian symbols, and 41 skeletons lying with their heads to the west and their feet to the east, the customary Christian method of burial in Western Europe. This followed the east-west alignment of churches, pointing to Palestine, from the belief that risen souls would face east on the 'Day of Judgement' when Jesus would descend to the Holy Land to pronounce the eternal fate of all people.

East Anglia was among the first parts of England colonised by the Anglo-Saxons, resulting into a lapse into paganism. In 590 Pope Gregory the Great despatched St. Augustine to bring Christianity to the Anglo-Saxons. Arriving in Kent Augustine began the evangelisation of England from Canterbury. King Redwald of East Anglia was unable to abandon his traditional beliefs, and set up Christian and pagan altars in his palace (traditionally said to have been at Rendlesham). Redwald is generally thought to have been the king buried at Sutton Hoo, suggesting that Nordic paganism held sway in Suffolk at the start of the seventh century. In about 630 the throne of East Anglia passed to one of Redwald's sons, Sigebehrt, a Christian, who invited Felix, a Burgundian bishop, to establish an organised church in East Anglia. The Christianisation of the region seems to have followed rapidly, since archaeological excavations have found that from this period onwards the dead were again buried in an east-west orientation.

In 869 Viking invaders defeated and slew Edmund, the last Anglo-Saxon king of East Anglia, supplanting him with a Viking called Guthrum, who accepted Christianity. By the twelfth century there was a tradition that Guthrum was buried at Hadleigh. There are stories that the foundations of an early building were uncovered to the south of Hadleigh church in the eighteenth and nineteenth centuries. These cannot be seen now, but if they were the remains of the church in which Guthrum was buried, this churchyard (pictured) has the longest continually documented history of any Christian burial ground in Suffolk.

In 918 Alfred the Great's son, Edward 'the Elder' conquered East Anglia, which was then absorbed into a wholly Christianised England. In 1086 the *Domesday Book* recorded over 350 churches in Suffolk, more than it listed for the rest of England put together. It therefore seems likely that there was a church in every town and village in the county by that date. It seems equally likely that these churches had surrounding churchyards. Nearly every church in Suffolk was enlarged or rebuilt between the twelfth and sixteenth centuries, but, even if a wholly new church replaced an older one, it normally remained in the same churchyard. It thus seems reasonable to assume that most parish churchyards in Suffolk have been used for burials since the later Anglo-Saxon era. (One exception is Walberswick, where the original parish church, near a tidal river, was threatened by a rise in the water level, and abandoned in 1473, when the present church was built further inland.)

The few latecomers among Suffolk towns, such as Orford and Newmarket, which came into existence in the twelfth and thirteenth centuries, were provided with churches and churchyards. The only omission was Needham Market, which developed in the thirteenth century, but remained part of the parish of Barking until 1907. The church in Needham Market High Street was a 'chapel of ease' to Barking, and never used for burials. (Local tradition holds that funerals processed along 'The Causeway', from the High Street to Barking church.) Because of its origins as a chapel of ease, this is the only medieval parish church in Suffolk aligned north-south, and lacking a churchyard.

In many churchyards stone crosses were erected to demonstrate the enclosure's holy nature and serve as a common memorial to those buried there. (It had been said that the dead must sleep within the shadow of the cross, which spreads its arms to protect the living and dead.) Suffolk's earliest churchyard memorial, in the broadest sense of the word, is the shaft of an Anglo-Saxon stone cross in St. Botolph's church at Iken. The *Anglo-Saxon Chronicle* records that St. Botolph built a monastery in East Anglia at 'Ikenho' in 654. This was later destroyed by the Vikings and never rebuilt. Archaeologists and historians suspected that Iken stood on the site of Ikenho, but could not prove this until 1977, when the church was burnt out in a fire. While investigating the damage Stanley West found a cross shaft within the fabric of the tower wall. This discovery suggested that Iken had been an important Anglo-Saxon religious centre. It is now believed that Iken church marks the site of Botolph's monastery and this cross was erected in his memory.

*Hessett*

*Hawstead*

*Brockley*

*Elmswell*

After the Reformation representations of the crucifixion were condemned as idolatrous and most churchyard crosses were destroyed. The most prominent surviving example in Suffolk stands by the churchyard gate at Hessett, and this has lost its head, which would probably have shown the crucifixion. Cross bases at Hawstead and Brockley may have been made by the same masons. One at Elmswell was restored in the Victorian era, when a new top, copying medieval survivals, was added.

In the Roman Empire burial inside a church building was originally an exclusive privilege, reserved for saints or martyrs. It gradually came to be permitted for the most important members of the wealthy or ruling classes. Members of this privileged elite, or their families, began to pay for monuments to be built in their honour inside the church. While interior monuments are outside the scope of this book, a thirteenth century example can be seen at Hawstead. Exterior monuments, which may be regarded as early churchyard memorials, can be seen on the south walls of the aisle of Eriswell church and the chancel of Great Barton. Stone arches sheltering stone coffins, these may have been built to house the remains of the people who paid for these parts of the church. It is possible that, for some uncertain reason, the ecclesiastical authorities would not permit the benefactor who paid for the work to be buried inside the church, so they were buried beside the church wall to ensure that their generosity was still remembered. As burial inside the church became increasingly acceptable from the fourteenth century monuments survive in increasing numbers, although, before the nineteenth century, most of these are to the higher clergy, the greater landowners, or the wealthy.

*Eriswell*                    *Great Barton*

As churchyards became filled with graves, new internments often unearthed previous burials. The southwest area of the abbey precinct at Bury St. Edmunds was set aside as the town burial ground, known as *The Great Churchyard*. By 1300 so many bones were being dug up here that Abbot Hugh Northwold ordered the construction of a charnel house where these could be stored. A lower chamber was a 'bone house' for skeletal remains, while a (long vanished) upper chamber contained a chapel. This passed out of use at the Reformation (after which unearthed bones were probably reinterred with minimal ceremony). It then passed through a variety of secular uses, including an alehouse and a blacksmith's shop, before falling into ruin. In the eighteenth century John Spink, a local banker, bought the ruin, and had it surrounded with elaborate wrought iron railings, intending to turn it into a family mausoleum. On his death the the Great Churchyard was purchased by James Oakes, another banker (who left a diary of local life). He sold it to the Borough Corporation, when the Charnel House became the focal point of the churchyard, on which prestige memorials were placed.

In 1386 a charnel house was built at Mildenhall. While Mildenhall is the largest parish in Suffolk, possessing one of the county's largest parish churches, the churchyard is comparatively small and may therefore have filled with burials at an early date, causing corpses to be unearthed more frequently. As at Bury, the lower chamber was a 'bone house'; an upper chamber contained a chapel dedicated to St. Michael. This, too, fell into ruin after the Reformation; in the Victorian era it was converted into a memorial to the Read family. (Picture at top of page 9.)

By the sixteenth century it was becoming increasingly common for people to draw up 'wills', to settle their affairs after their death. Early Suffolk wills have been studied in great depth by two admirable local historians, Peter Northeast and Judith Middleton-Stewart, whose recent passing was a great loss. Some testators request that memorials be placed over their graves. While such references are the exception rather than the rule, they occur frequently enough  to suggest that it might not have been unusual to see gravestones in churchyards. In 1502 John Coote of Bury St. Edmunds requested that wooden crosses be placed at the head and foot of his grave, carved with prayers for his soul. In 1512 Thomas Kerych of Walberswick specified that he wanted 'a gravestone of lime and stone two feet high' near the churchyard path to the holy water stoup. At Reydon in 1537 William Haggs asked to be buried near the church porch under a memorial 'heaved above the ground with masons' craft three quarters of a yard [27 inches] and pinned up with stone'.

Suffolk's earliest surviving churchyard memorials can be found at Hessett. These bear inscriptions (now difficult to decipher) to John and Robert Bacon, and their wives, Margery and Isabel. John Bacon, who died in 1513, was a wealthy sheep farmer who organised the building of Hessett and several other Suffolk churches. His son Robert left an increased fortune on his death in 1548. (Robert's son, Nicholas, became Keeper of the Great Seal to Elizabeth I; Nicholas's son was Francis Bacon, Lord Chancellor of England and one of the most important writers and philosophers of the Elizabethan and Jacobean age. Another of Nicholas's descendants acquired the title of baronet: his descendants still live in Suffolk.)

In 1520 John Ponder, a wealthy clothier at Lavenham, commissioned an elaborate churchyard memorial, with carvings that resembled the church's exterior decorations. This was later moved inside the church, so that it is often mistaken for an indoor memorial. The Bacons and John Ponder had contributed money to the churches, yet they might not quite have

qualified for an inside burial. These memorials may have survived because they were made from large stone blocks, which were less likely to be destroyed by the weather, or submerged by vegetation (and difficult to demolish or remove).

This elaborate construction on the south wall of Ringsfield church commemorates Nicholas Garneys of Redisham Hall, who died in 1599. Nicholas and his family are represented on a monumental brass in the centre of the memorial: one of the few surviving examples of its kind to have been made for the outside of a church, (copied from his grandfather's memorial brass at Kenton). Above this there is a passage from 2 Timothy 4: 7-8, perhaps illustrating the Protestant emphasis on the teaching of the word. The memorial is topped by a mermaid, the Garneys family crest. Precisely why the memorial stands outside the church is unclear: one theory is that Nicholas Garneys had a doctrinal difference with the rector; another possibility is that it was too large to fit inside the church!

# CHEST TOMBS

Churchyard monuments survive in increasing numbers from the seventeenth century onwards. While it is possible that older memorials were worn away by the weather, destroyed during periods of religious intolerance, or removed to make way for newer ones, the appearance of so many after this date suggests that these were being made in greater quantities and to higher standards of workmanship than ever before.

There are several possible explanations for this. The interiors of churches may have had been filled with memorials, and every space under church floors occupied by burials. (The loss of many churches at the Reformation would have increased pressure on those that remained in use.) Thus the parish elite had no alternative but to be buried outside the church. By the seventeenth century England's population had returned to the level that it had reached before the Black Death, and was continuing to increase. This obviously caused a growth in the number of deaths and burials. As had happened in the Great Churchyard in Bury St. Edmunds, it became increasingly difficult to lay a dead person to rest without disturbing a previous interment. People may have feared that their remains, too, would be disturbed by later burials: an obvious way to prevent this was to place a memorial over their grave. Hygiene may have been a consideration, as monuments would prevent decaying corpses from being exhumed.

The historian W. G. Hoskins advanced a thesis that there was a 'great rebuilding' in England between 1570 and 1640, when many houses were constructed on a more substantial scale, to increasingly sophisticated designs. The same impulses that may have caused people to build new houses: greater prosperity (at least for some members of society); increased availability of building materials; the impulse for 'conspicuous consumption', and the aspiration to express individuality, may have extended into death, with a greater desire to advertise one's status with a churchyard memorial. One aspect of 'the great rebuilding' was the concept of what would now be called 'privacy': throughout the middle ages even the greatest noblemen shared their mansions and castles with their servants and retainers. During the late Tudor and early Stuart era people began to construct intimate houses, where families or individuals could maintain a separate space. The desire for more privacy in life may have led to the desire for more privacy in death.

While there was a reaction against many traditional forms of religious observance after the Reformation, churchyard burials normally continued to be oriented east-west. This may have been out of convention, or because it was easier and more practical to continue to dig graves in alignment with a pattern that had been preferred for several hundred years

From the second quarter of the century 'Chest Tombs' become common. So called for the obvious reason that they resemble rectangular chests, early examples are often to prominent members of the community, and stand close to the church, even against the church wall. An early chest tomb beside Groton church was made for Adam Winthrop, the lord of the manor, who died in 1623. Adam was a leading member of the Puritan

movement in Suffolk and Essex; his son, John, led a Puritan migration to New England in North America, becoming governor of Massachusetts. The Winthrop family's role in establishing the English colonies in New England has turned Groton into a centre of transatlantic pilgrimage, and it is regularly visited by travellers from the U.S.A.

The two earliest surviving memorials in the Great Churchyard in Bury St. Edmunds, to John and Edward Bourne, dated 1637 and 1638, stand northwest of St. Mary's church.

A chest tomb by the nave doorway at Theberton was made for John Fenn, the son of William Fenn, the rector, who was ejected during the Civil War for loyalty to Charles I. The inscription (perhaps intentionally humorous) reads:

*Here is a stone to sitt upon under which lies in hopes to rise to ye day of blisse and happinesse honest John Fenn the son of William Fenn, Clarke & late rector of this parish being turned out of this living and sequestred for his loyalty to the late King Charles the First. Hee departed this life the 22 day of October anno dom 1678.*

The Fox family memorial at Stradbroke is rather lower, but much wider than a normal chest tomb, and protected by copper sheets, some of which bear Latin inscriptions describing the family's achievements and how they left money in trust for distribution of bread to the people of Stradbroke (and to maintain their memorial).

This memorial to William Sancroft, Archbishop of Canterbury, stands beside Fressingfield church. Born in Fressingfield in 1617, William Sancroft became a member of Cambridge University, and remained sympathetic to the royal family during the Civil War and Commonwealth. Charles II appointed him Dean of St. Paul's in London and then Archbishop of Canterbury. He crowned Charles II's successor, James II, after which he found himself compelled to oppose James II's plans to restore Roman Catholicism to England: he was imprisoned, but popular sympathy soon led to his release. Ultimately James II was overthrown in favour of the Dutch King William III. Despite his opposition to James II's policies, William Sancroft believed he still owed loyalty to the king whom he had crowned and retired from public office to Fressingfield, where he commissioned a memorial to stand outside the church. The desire to erect churchyard memorials obviously spread across all shades of the religious and political spectrum: while the Winthrop family and William Sancroft had diametrically opposite attitudes to Christianity and the Stuart dynasty, they both erected expensive memorials beside their parish church.

During the seventeenth and eighteenth centuries most churchyard memorials were ordered on an ad hoc basis from a local carpenter, builder or mason, who (hopefully) was sufficiently literate to add an inscription. Carpenters and builders often doubled as undertakers, with the result that early churchyard memorials resemble items of

furniture or display architectural details. A tomb at Little Saxham with corner pilasters that look like table legs (*page 14*), was made for Charles Crofts, of the long demolished Little Saxham Hall, who died in 1737. It stands against the Crofts family memorial chapel, possibly because there was no room inside. The upper face bears a lengthy inscription and a cartouche showing the Crofts coat of arms.

Thomas Gainsborough, the most famous native of Sudbury, was buried in Kew church in London. His parents, John and Mary Gainsborough (nee Burroughs), his sister Mary, and several members of his family were buried under this chest tomb in All Saints' churchyard in Sudbury. Again the corner pilasters resemble table legs: in the centre there is a carving of a tapestry of the sort that may have been displayed at funerals, depicting a winged skull (representing the swiftness of time) wearing a laurel wreath (a symbol of victory: in this case the triumph of death).

Another chest tomb at All Saints' churchyard in Sudbury. The pilasters at the sides bear carvings of flowers, reminders of death as they are perishable. As often happens, ivy can take root within the stonework: if not checked this can pull the monument apart.

Roundels resembling furniture decorations or drawer handles appear on this chest tomb in the Great Churchyard in Bury St. Edmunds. The inscription at the top honours Lieutenant Colonel Thomas Hockley, who died in 1804, aged 48, saying that he was known as 'the soldier's friend'. While this implies dedication to improving the welfare of those under his command, I have been unable to find out much about his career.

The Robinson family memorial in the Great Churchyard in Bury St. Edmunds suggests the work of a builder rather than a carpenter. Henry Robinson, one of the people buried under this memorial, was the father of Henry Crabb Robinson, a journalist during the Napoleonic wars, who has been described as the first war correspondent. Although Henry Crabb Robinson was buried in Highgate Cemetery in London, he is mentioned on this memorial.

A. E. Thurlow, in Ixworth High Street, a long established local firm, operating from a former blacksmith's forge, demonstrates the tradition of combining a builder's or practical tradesman's and undertaker's business.

# HEADSTONES AND THE SYMBOLISM OF DEATH

From the final quarter of the seventeenth century graves began to be marked by 'headstones' placed against the deceased's head, and smaller 'footstones' at the feet. A large 'bodystone' covering the grave sometimes lay between these. It may have been that a general increase in prosperity left people with more money to spend on such items; fashion may have played a part, as the middle and lower classes imitated the churchyard monuments of the upper class. It may also have been thought that these would safeguard the burial: a sexton might have been less inclined to disturb a marked grave, if just because the stones would get in the way of his spade.

Headstones were decorated with instantly recognisable motifs, or 'symbols of mortality', which would be understood by the literate and illiterate alike. Some of the most popular were skulls and long bones, often combined to form the familiar 'skull and crossbones'. Hour glasses symbolised the passage of time. Sexton's tools, such as spades and pickaxes, appeared because these were used to dig graves. Scythes cut corn and cleared vegetation from churchyards, their symbolism is shown by the expressions 'grim reaper', and the phrase 'cut down in his prime'. A snake curled into a circle biting its own tail ('serpent of eternity') symbolised infinity as it had no beginning or end. Coffins are self-explanatory. While these ceased to be fashionable during the nineteenth century, a ubiquitous symbol, which has proved rather more popular and long lasting, is the cherub, represented as a head flying on wings. The commonest single headstone image throughout the seventeenth and eighteenth centuries, it could signify the soul rising from the grave, a guardian spirit or a watchful angel, a rather more optimistic emblem than a skull and crossbones!

The earliest dated 'headstone' I have found in Suffolk stands in a row of gravestones roughly north of Pakenham church. In memory of 'John Acer, Gent' who died in February 1677, it bears a naïve carving of a skull between two floral ornaments.

Memorials dated 1683 and 1684 on the south of Great Bradley parish church show the transition from 'chest tombs' to 'body stones' bordered by headstones and footstones. One bodystone displays a skeleton wrapped in a shroud, another shows drapery, representing a shroud drawn around a body. Smaller examples cover children's graves.

This 'bodystone' between a head and foot stone in Cavendish churchyard looks attractive covered in moss. The inscription has been worn away, but on these, and the examples at Great Bradley, the main inscription is on the exterior, westward facing, side of the larger headstone. A smaller inscription (often just the deceased's initials) might be found on the eastward facing side of the footstone.

Coffin shaped bodystones at Cavendish.

During the twentieth century footstones were often moved westward to stand against the headstone. This is due in part to the development of the mechanical lawnmower which is easier to manoeuvre around a single gravestone than between two adjoining stones. The footstone could be covered by soil and vegetation, so it might therefore be practical to

place it against a headstone. Modern sensibilities might regard an even churchyard with rows of regular gravestones as more pleasing than an irregular churchyard with an uneven surface and a mixture of memorials. At Cavendish, again, we see a row of footstones standing against the headstones.

Badley is an underpopulated parish, and the church (now in the care of the Churches Conservation Trust) which is one of the most remote in Suffolk, was never restored or modernised in the nineteenth or twentieth centuries. The churchyard, too, has not been disturbed, and the

headstones and footstones in the churchyard still stand apart. Two ways of establishing whether or not a gravestone is in its original location is to look for a footstone to the west, or see if it faces eastwards: gravestones facing north or south have often been moved from their original locations.

Three small headstones and footstones near the churchyard gate at Badley mark the burials of children and infants. Early deaths such as these were often laid to rest on the edge of the churchyard.

A group of memorials in the Great Churchyard in Bury St. Edmunds, showing some representative types of eighteenth and early nineteenth century designs. Sometimes a bodystone on its own would be placed over a burial. One general characteristic of the headstones and footstones are the gently rounded,

or irregular shaped tops. Rectangular tops are uncommon. One headstone shows two rounded tops: these often commemorate a husband and wife.

Dated headstones become increasingly common from the third decade of the seventeenth century. This headstone, bearing the date 1690, by the east wall of the Great Churchyard in Bury St. Edmunds, shows a cherub's head. It was moved from the area south of the Cathedral during the 1950's.

This headstone dated 1693, in the porch of Wickhambrook church, is two feet high. Commemorating a vicar of the nearby parish of Denham, it is circled by a wreath of fruit and flowers, as seen in many contemporary paintings. While aesthetically pleasing, they are reminders of death, as they are perishable. The analogy is emphasised by the skull at the top of the stone.

Two headstones at Little Saxham, dated 1697, show skulls wearing ruff collars (by then an archaic fashion) and cherub's heads. They are part of a row of early headstones running parallel to the south wall of the nave, suggesting that these were moved from elsewhere in the churchyard.

A headstone by the charnel house in the Great Churchyard in Bury St. Edmunds, is dated 1698. Skulls, crossed bones, hour glasses and cherub's heads surround an inscription (a commonplace in funerary art) that the dead were once living, like the reader, and that the reader too will die.

> Good people all, as you pas by,
> Looke round, see how corpses do lye,
> For as you are somtime ware we
> And as we are so must you be.

The cherubs might convey an optimistic hope of resurrection.

Three headstones at Withersfield are dated 1699: the central one features wreathes of flowers; the other two show what appear to be 'skulls and crossbones', but a close examination of the left hand one shows this to be a crossed spade and scythe, and that on the right is a crossed trumpet and torch.

These headstones in the Great Churchyard in Bury St. Edmunds show spaces for inscriptions, sadly worn away, surrounded by scrollwork, cherubs, skulls, longbones and hour glasses. In the third the space is heart shaped, perhaps symbolic of charity.

This headstone at Aldeburgh shows a crossed pick and shovel, and a skull between two cherubs heads (one partially destroyed): at the foot of the stone there are the frequently quoted Latin words 'memento mori'; which can be translated as 'remember you will (or must) die', or 'prepare to die'. (There is a story that when Roman Emperors appeared on state occasions a slave walked alongside them repeating this to remind them that death even came to all, no matter how powerful.)

Three gravestones at Lavenham show sophisticated workmanship: one displays drapery; another skulls and scrollwork; a third depicts skulls and cherubs over a wreath. Similar designs can be seen at Alpheton and St. Gregory's churchyard in Sudbury: perhaps a local craftsman or workshop produced memorials of exceptional quality.

Familiar images of death at Great Barton.

A sequence at Ramsholt includes a skull with a spade and a coffin, and an imagined example of the heraldry of death: crossed longbones on a shield.

A row of headstones at Horringer show cherubs, skulls and flowers. The build-up of soil has covered the lower sections, while their weight has caused them to fall in extreme angles.

A cherub and skulls within elaborate scrollwork at Dalham.

Cherubs and hourglasses at Little Whelnetham.

Cherubs within flowers at Worlington.

Most of the headstones in St. Mary's churchyard at Newmarket have been cleared away, but one of the few preserved examples shows a cherub, skulls, hourglasses, and three crossed 'symbols of mortality': longbones, a spade and pickaxe, and a coffin and scythe.

Three dimensional carvings of a cherub, a skull and an hourglass at Barningham.

Sexton's tools, a coffin, an hourglass and a 'serpent of eternity' at Burgh.

An hour glass, a spade and pick at Dallinghoo.

A coffin with the lid beginning to rise, a symbol of resurrection, at Acton.

Crossed longbones between two skulls at Peasenhall.

Sometimes hour glasses appear with wings, as in these two examples at Flempton, representing the expression 'time flies', the swiftness of time and the onset of death.

At Yoxford a cherub appears with two arrows, representing death, as these are fatal weapons which come quickly.

While skulls and bones appear on many gravestones, entire skeletons are less common, perhaps because they were difficult and time consuming (and therefore expensive) to carve. In 1699 they were portrayed holding spades at Elmswell.

Two headstones at St. Nicholas's church in Ipswich (*left*) and Wetheringsett parish church (*right*) are so similar that they were probably carved by the same mason. They show an articulated skeleton rising from a coffin, pointing to a book with an arrow (a fatal weapon), presumably a reference to the day of judgement when the dead will rise and their actions will be listed for or against them.

At Great Thurlow death, in the form of a skeleton waving an arrow, seizes a child in a cradle, despite the protests of another figure, either the mother, or a personification of 'Time'. The inscription says the headstone commemorates Mary Traylen who died in 1797, aged 30, and one of her children who died in infancy.

At Brent Eleigh a fantastic portrayal of the triumph of death appears on the east face of a chest tomb. A skeleton wears a laurel wreath (a classical symbol of victory) and holds an hour glass in one hand while his other arm rests on a spade. This must be one of the most spectacular examples of gravestone art in England.

It would be difficult to overstate the influence of classical culture on the educated and upper classes in Britain during the eighteenth and nineteenth centuries. Classical languages and literature were the major subject of study at 'Grammar Schools' and Oxford and Cambridge Universities. Most clergymen were well versed in Greek and Latin literature and saw nothing wrong in bringing classical imagery into the church, since this affirmed knowledge and reason, basic tenets of the Christian faith.

Travel to classical ruins was fashionable among the gentry and aristocracy (as well as aspiring artists, architects and sculptors). At Heveningham and Ickworth the Vanneck and Hervey families commissioned their country mansions in a classical style; after Catholic Emancipation the Roman Catholic Church in Bury St. Edmunds was built with the appearance of a Greek temple. (The Bury St. Edmunds Corn Exchange, too, would be erected with a classical portico.) While a classical education and travel to

Greece and Italy was beyond the means of most of the population, translations of classical literature were accessible to literate members of the middle, and even lower, classes: they clearly influenced Robert Bloomfield 'the Suffolk poet'. Prints and drawings of classical monuments circulated widely. Inside churches the gentry and aristocracy would commission classical tombs with lengthy Latin inscriptions, sometimes with statues portraying them in Roman togas. Thus it was inevitable that churchyard memorials would display classical influences.

Several Roman Emperors commemorated their achievements with obelisks, and these again enjoyed a vogue in the eighteenth century (one contemporary example stands in Chequer Square in Bury St. Edmunds). These could often be erected in appreciation of what might have been regarded as a distinguished career (a truly enormous example was erected in honour of Frederick Hervey, the 'Earl Bishop' at Ickworth). This obelisk at Dalham, over twenty feet high, is Suffolk's tallest churchyard memorial. It was erected in honour of James Affleck, the third baronet of Dalham Hall, who was colonel of the 16th Light Dragoons and became a general at 66. (I have found out little about James Affleck's military career beyond the fact that he fought in the American War of Independence: at that time military posts could be purchased, and promotion could be a matter of seniority.)

The scallop shell was used to embellish alcoves or niches. (It was also a crossover from medieval imagery, as the badge of pilgrims making the trip to Santiago de Compostella in Spain, in which context it appeared on the west front of St. James's church (now the cathedral) in Bury St. Edmunds.) Scallop shells and cherubs appear at Ickworth (*left*); at Cavendish (*right*) one appears with cherubs and flowers. (Perhaps it was not so widely known that it was also a symbol of the goddess Venus.)

The sarcophagus, a large stone memorial, was made by the Ancient Greeks and Etruscans. Sarcophagi became common among the Romans during the second century. This example at Acton, commemorating the Kedington family, bears Latin inscriptions. (While classical sarcophagi contained the remains of the dead, in churchyards the deceased were normally buried underneath the memorial.)

Classically inspired sarcophagi in the Great Churchyard in Bury St. Edmunds.

A row of monuments in classical style at Syleham.

Cremation was practiced in Athens, and was common across the Roman Empire during the first and second centuries A.D. The ashes of the deceased were stored in funerary urns, which became symbolic of death or mourning. Paradoxically, while burning a dead body would usually have been regarded with abhorrence in eighteenth and early nineteenth century England, cinerary urns became popular funerary motifs. Some larger memorials were topped by stone urns with carved flames coming from the apex. This example is in St. Mary's churchyard in Woodbridge. (It commemorates James Pulham. Another native of Woodbridge with this name invented an artificial stone called 'Pulhamite' which became a fashionable garden ornament. It has sometimes been thought that this is a memorial to the inventor, but there was no connection between the two people beyond the fact that they shared the same name.)

A headstone at Bildeston shows an urn and vases on a classical altar.

A flaming torch or taper represented life and energy: its continued appeal is shown by the torch carried by athletes at the start of the Olympic Games (an event initiated by the ancient Greeks). Torches were turned upside down and pressed to the ground or immersed in water to extinguish them: thus an inverted torch signified the end of life. Urns with inverted torches appear at Great Barton (*top*), Acton (*left*) and Redgrave (*right*).

Cherubs with inverted torches and an arrow at Yoxford.

This vignette, also at Yoxford, of cherubs garlanding a funerary urn, may have been copied from an engraving.

A scene at Glemsford, perhaps inspired by prints of classical ruins, shows a child sitting among monuments (including an urn), either studying or writing on a tablet.

A tree with low hanging branches symbolised mourning (hence the expression 'weeping willow'). At St. Mary's church at Bungay one hangs over an urn.

'Mourning figures' standing over graves were popular images in Greek and Roman commemorative art. At Stanstead one such mourner standing beside a weeping willow contemplates a sarcophagus. (Fitting the elements of the design into a limited space at the top of the headstone has caused some errors with perspective, as the tree is smaller than the mourner.)

This stylised portrayal of a grief stricken mourning figure beside a distinctly Roman sarcophagus at Chilton honours Thomas Creaton, steward of Chilton Hall for 36 years.

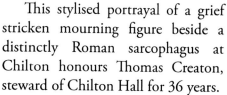

A homely vignette at Hawstead shows a mourning figure weeping into the drapery that covers an urn. A skull appears in the corner.

At Stoke by Nayland a mourner buries her face in a large handkerchief, in front of a sarcophagus displaying a 'skull and crossbones'. While handkerchiefs have restricted uses now, in Classical times, and in Britain up to the nineteenth century these were regarded as important fashion accessories.

At Chedburgh mourners in theatrical looking classical costumes stand beside an urn, wiping their tears away with large handkerchiefs: one holds an inverted torch, which still emits smoke.

While pyramids are commonly associated with Ancient Egypt, they were absorbed into Greek and Roman culture ('pyramid' is a Greek word: the ancient Egyptians called these structures 'mer' meaning 'places of ascendance'). Alexander the Great conquered Egypt, after which it was ruled by a Greek Ptolemaic dynasty, before being incorporated into the Roman Empire. As the  largest memorials to the dead ever constructed, their symbolism would have been clearly apparent. One representation in St. Mary's churchyard at Bungay warns 'reader prepare for eternity'.

A tearful cherub by a pyramid at Little Saxham

A headstone at Acton shows a child perhaps meditating upon death and decay, surrounded by several classical motifs, including a broken altar and a shattered pyramid.

From the eighteenth century a book, representing the Bible, began to appear on headstones. This would have been an obvious emblem of Christianity, especially to Nonconformists who treasured 'the word' as the central part of their belief. It could also symbolise prayer, knowledge, or the record of the person's life: open books are still popular gravestone motifs.

The 'Hand of God' appears from a cloud at Little Cornard, pointing to the Bible with the stern warning 'read, mark, learn'.

At Kersey a Bible appears alongside an hourglass and a 'serpent of eternity'.

At Wangford (near Southwold) a cherub curves its wings to admit the picture of a book.

At Reydon (*left*) a Bible floats between two cherubs, while at Halesworth (*right*) it stands on an altar, beside a cherub.

Sometimes the Bible displays a warning or comforting message. At Holy Trinity Church in Bungay, a Bible, between a flaming torch and a trumpet, symbolising life and resurrection, reads 'O death where is thy sting, O grave thy victory' (1 Corinthians, 15: 55).

At Peasenhall (*left*) a book between two cherubs displays the phrase 'memento mori'. At Halesworth (*right*) the book stands over an open grave, from which bones protrude, presenting an English translation of this phrase: 'prepare to die'. The corner of the page is turned over, to symbolise memory or remind the reader of a message that must be returned to. (The habit of bending corners to mark a page is a shocking way to mistreat a book: it is more sensible to use a bookmark.)

God's 'all seeing eye' (also known as 'the Eye of Providence') appears on its own at Clare (*left*), and with two cherubs at Great Cornard (*right*). The design might be recognised from U.S. dollar bills (as it forms part of the seal of the U.S.A.). Since the late eighteenth century this has also been a symbol of Freemasonry. The analogy appears in Psalms 33: 13 and 34: 15; Proverbs 15: 3; Jeremiah 24: 6; Ezekiel 5: 11 and Amos 9: 8.

At Beccles 'God's all-seeing eye' appears alongside a cherub's head and a Bible bearing two phrases: 'let all mortal flesh keep silence' (a rephrasing of Habakkuk 2: 20 that became the title line of a hymn) and 'God is judge himself' (Psalm 50:6).

Sometimes a person, usually a woman, was shown 'searching the scriptures'. At Leiston the text 'I know that my redeemer liveth' (Job 19: 25) faces her line of vision rather than the viewer's.

God's 'all-seeing eye' often watches the women searching the scriptures: at Hawstead (*left*) she is a rather dumpy figure; at Great Saxham (*centre*) she sits before an urn; at Groton (*right*) the scene is surrounded by a 'serpent of eternity'.

Hope is compared to an anchor in Hebrews, 6: 19 ('this hope we have as an anchor of the soul'). This passage has become a popular spiritual metaphor in Britain, perhaps because of national maritime traditions. Hope is often personified as a woman holding an anchor in her right hand while pointing heavenwards with her left. At Aldringham she is surrounded by the inscription 'we hope to meet in heaven'.

The largest of three personifications of Hope is in St. Gregory's churchyard at Sudbury (*left*). There are smaller representations at Little Cornard (*centre*) and by the east wall of the Great Churchyard in Bury St. Edmunds (*right*), where she stands underneath God's 'all-seeing' eye.

At Brome Hope rests on a solid object: could this be a rock, symbolising refuge, strength and constancy (Matthew 7: 24-5; 16: 17), or a coil of rope? This headstone was set up during the Napoleonic wars, when the British navy achieved great prestige, which may explain the scene's rather nautical appearance.

At Horringer a classically influenced portrayal of Hope resembles Britannia.

At Rushbrooke Hope kneels beside a classical funerary urn partly concealed by drapery, from which a skull protrudes.

'Faith, Hope and Charity' (1 Corinthians 13: 13) is one of the best known Biblical expressions. In St. Margaret's churchyard at Lowestoft, roughly northeast of the church, Hope holds her anchor, Faith clings to the cross, while Charity nurtures a child.

St. Paul describes the resurrection of the dead in preparation for the 'Day of Judgement' in powerful imagery: 'We shall not all sleep, but we shall all be changed, for in a moment, in the twinkling of an eye, at the last trump, for the trumpet shall sound, and the dead shall be raised incorruptible' (1 Corinthians, 15: 51-2). 'The Lord himself shall descend from Heaven with a shout, with the voice of the archangel, and with the trump of God; and the dead in Christ shall rise first' (1 Thessalonians 4: 16). An angel or archangel blowing a trumpet to raise the dead would be a most appropriate scene for a gravestone, although this cherub blowing a trumpet at Walberswick looks like a child with a toy musical instrument.

In the Great Churchyard in Bury St Edmunds a cherub with a trumpet points to a Bible, although his nude figure rather detracts from the decorum of the scene.

There is a rather more powerful image of an angel blowing the last trump at Thornham Magna.

At Brandeston an angel with pitifully small wings flies over a small cloud: it is hard to tell if he is flying on the cloud, or holding on in desperation.

At Edwardstone the resurrection of the dead is portrayed as a hand from heaven holding a scroll over a churchyard tomb, perhaps referring to images of 'the last days': 'all the host of heaven shall be dissolved and the heavens shall be rolled together as a scroll' (Isaiah 34: 4); 'The heaven departed as a scroll when it is rolled together' (Revelation 7: 14).

Resurrection again appears at Stanstead as a human soul ascending to heaven. It flies from a church, surrounded by miniature gravestones, to a classical looking paradise, where a shady tree hangs over an urn.

Biblical scenes and figures on headstones would have required skilled and delicate craftsmanship to carve, which would be sadly prone to deteriorate with the weather. When I visited Brome churchyard in 2009 I noticed a group of churchyard memorials covered by undergrowth. On a return visit in 2011 I found that churchyard clearance had removed the vegetation, which may have preserved this portrayal of Moses with the Ten Commandments (Exodus 20: 1-17; 32: 15-19).

The weather has not been too kind to these carvings of the Sacrifice of Isaac (Genesis 22: 1-19) in the parish churchyards at Ixworth (*left*) and Clare (*right*). This scene might have been chosen as it showed total submission to the will of God. It may also represent God's mercy, since it shows the moment when the angel tells Abraham to stop; or God's promise, since God rewarded Abraham for his obedience by pledging a great future for his descendants. The episode has also been interpreted as a portent of the sacrifice of Jesus.

The story of how Jesus spoke to the Samaritan woman at Jacob's Well, (John 4: 1-42), a rather more pleasant story than that of the sacrifice of Isaac, appears at the United Reformed Church at Clare (*left*) and Southwold (*right*). This charming episode may have been chosen for its immediacy, as an unexpected meeting with Jesus who gives his teachings to an ordinary woman in an everyday encounter.

A charming series of gravestones on the south side of St. Margaret's churchyard at Lowestoft. Comparatively small, with short simple inscriptions, they display various 'symbols of mortality' in a naïve style that can be quite appealing. An early example, dated 1678, with a crudely carved border, shows a childishly carved 'skull and crossbones', but most date from the later eighteenth or early nineteenth century. In some classically inspired designs cherubs display books or scrolls, sometimes reclining on urns or sarcophagi. They might be the productions of local masons or craftsmen who created gravestones to order before mechanisation became the norm in the Victorian era.

This gravestone, at Carlton Colville, resembles some of those at Lowestoft. It may represent the souls of the departed ascending to heaven.

Similar examples of naïve art can be seen at Pakefield, south of Lowestoft (now part of the Lowestoft conurbation).

More gravestones showing naïvely carved symbols of mortality can be found at Southwold. Were these productions of the same masons who worked at Lowestoft, or another local school of craftsmen?

Bells might seem to be an appropriate gravestone symbol, as they call people to church and are sounded at funerals, yet they seldom appear on headstones in Suffolk before the twentieth century. Nevertheless some early headstones which do display bells are of unusual interest. At Hinderclay a headstone displays a bell among a variety of 'symbols of mortality'. It is strangely co-incidental that this church is known for *The Hinderclay Gotch*, a two gallon pitcher presented in 1724 to store beer for the bell ringers (featured on the village sign). The inscription has vanished, so we cannot know whom the gravestone commemorates, but it is

tempting to speculate that it was erected for the person who bought the 'gotch' or one of the bell ringers who drank from it.

A memorial at Copdock (*left*) honouring John Marven, composer of several ringing cycles. He belonged to the 'Society of College Youths', one of England's oldest bellringing clubs. The design is copied from his membership certificate. A headstone at Southwold (*right*) bears the worn inscription, 'In

memory of John Naunton, late of Ipswich, bell ringer and campanologist who died April 12 1824, aged 47 years'. He was a ringer at St. Mary le Tower church in Ipswich. (A bell ringer rings bells, while a campanologist studies them.) These headstones share a connection, for a board in the bell ringers' chamber at Lavenham records how John Naunton called the changes when one of John Marven's composition was rung there.

At Bildeston an angel sounding a bell commemorates John Simpson, another bell ringer.

John Pettitt's gravestone stands near the gatekeeper's lodge in the public cemetery in Friars Road at Hadleigh. Census returns record him as an innkeeper and brewer in Angel Street in Hadleigh: the 1861 census names the Inn where he was landlord as the *Eight Bells*, which still operates in the town: a most appropriate pub name! The inscription records:

In memory of John Pettitt, a great campanologist, died April 28 1872, aged 73.

*In many changes rung, I often took my stand,*
*My final change has come, to quit this sinful land,*
*So when the bells you hear, remember me again,*
*And hope that I am gone where joys for ever reign.*

Robert Arthur Bridges' headstone at Fornham St. Martin shows that he was a keen bellringer in his home parish and at the Norman Tower (the cathedral bell tower) in Bury St. Edmunds. The *Bury Free Press* of 28 April 1934 published some interesting recollections of his life. The memorial says he was a bell ringer for 56 years, but this may be an understatement, for a board in the nave of the church records how, on 14 May 1928 and 1929 peals of Bob Major were rung to honour his 76th and 77th birthdays, and his record of over sixty years as a ringer.

This gravestone in the modern cemetery in Shimpling Road in Hartest leaves no doubt as to Ranald Clouston's claim to fame. Born in Lavenham, he was an engineer by profession, and a dedicated bell ringer and campanologist by calling. As technical adviser to the Council for the Care of Churches he helped to conserve and repair church bells and ringing equipment across the British Isles. He wrote many studies on the subject, including a popular handbook on Suffolk church bells, receiving the M.B.E. for his services in this area.

*Father Time* appears on headstones at Brome (*left*) and Burgate (*right*). He was a conflation of two mythical figures from the classical era: *Chronos* and *Chronus* (also known as *Saturn*). Chronos, the personification of time, bore a long beard (symbolising old age). Chronus/Saturn overthrew *Uranus* to end primordial chaos: among other attributes he was the God of the Harvest. He carried a scythe, the symbol of the harvest, and the weapon with which he overthrew Uranus. The hour glass, a medieval invention, was an afterthought to a portrayal. Another of Father Time's attributes is a prominent forelock of hair, from the expression 'to take time by the forelock' (meaning to seize the moment).

At Stanningfield Father Time stands over a skull.

There is a classically influenced portrayal of Father Time with an urn at Yoxford (*left*); at the United Reformed Church in Haverhill (*right*) the setting includes a 'skull and crossbones'.

Suffolk's long-standing maritime tradition has inspired some impressive churchyard memorials. At Walberswick a cutter rigged ship appears on the gravestone of Elizabeth, wife of Thomas Archer, who died in 1781. James Maggs' *Handbook of Southwold Shipping* records that Thomas Archer was master of the *Dunwich*, a sixty ton vessel built in Ipswich: is this pictured here?

At Southwold Captain John Steele is commemorated by an angel blowing a trumpet over a ship *(left)*. Is the angel calling drowned sailors to the Day of Judgement, or protecting the ship? It is unfortunate that this outstanding example of gravestone art has deteriorated so badly: it can only be hoped that it receives conservation treatment, or is moved where it will not be exposed to the elements. Also at Southwold, a schooner appears on the gravestone of James Palmer, a master mariner *(centre)*. Benjamin Herrington's memorial *(right)* shows a fishing boat: the sail bears the number LT835: research in the Lowestoft branch of the Suffolk Record Office shows that this was the longshore boat *Rapid*, which he co-owned with four other fishermen.

At Aldeburgh the headstone of William Job Chatten, a Trinity House pilot, displays a three masted ship in full sail.

Headstones in Lowestoft public cemetery, at the junction of Rotterdam Road and Normanston Drive, display several poignant scenes, such as a fishing boat in sail on Robert Norman's memorial (plot 4, grave 251). The Ratcliffe family monument shows a lifeboat, perhaps symbolising a safe passage to the next world, or the saving grace of Jesus (plot 9, grave 343). Benjamin Thomas Butcher's gravestone (plot 8, grave 79) displays a particularly fine scene of a steam-powered fishing lugger.

James Barker's headstone in Pakefield churchyard, dated 1911, shows a contemporary fishing boat that used both sails (practical if there were favourable tides and currents) and steam power (more expensive, but guaranteed to move the ship in bad weather). The ship is surrounded by a representation of a 'life saver' probably alluding to the redeeming power of faith. The epitaph, from a popular hymn of the time, reads:

*I am resting so sweetly in Jesus now,*
*I sail the wide sea no more,*
*The tempest may sweep o'er the wild stormy deep,*
*I am safe where the storm come no more.*

Shotley church stands further from the village it was built to serve than any other church in Suffolk, in a churchyard which commands some of the most spectacular views of any burial ground in the county, as this scene shows. Between 1905 and 1976 Shotley was the home of H.M.S. Ganges, a training establishment for boys aged 15 or 16 who wished to serve in the Royal Navy. (There is now a museum dedicated to H.M.S. Ganges at Shotley Marina.) Sadly, it was inevitable that some of the boys would die of illness or in accidents before they completed their training: many such fatalities were buried in an eastern extension of Shotley churchyard under specially designed headstones.

# 'TOOLS OF THE TRADE' OCCUPATIONAL HEADSTONES

Some headstones display designs that are connected with the deceased person's former occupation. John Catchpole, a wagoner who died in 1792, is buried in Palgrave churchyard. The headstone shows a wagon drawn by six horses; the epitaph reads:

> My horses have done running
> My waggon is decayed
> And now in the dust my body is lay'd
> My whip is worn out, my work it is done,
> And now I'm brought here to my last home.

Samuel Croft's headstone stands near the churchyard gate at Blyford. Only 21 when he died, the *Ipswich Journal* of 19 May 1849 says he was the youngest son of James Croft, landlord of the nearby Queen's Head pub. We cannot know if he was a ploughman (as this memorial suggests), but this is a lovely representation of horses in agriculture.

This carving appears on the side of a coffin shaped chest tomb of John Chilton, a gypsy horse dealer, in Kesgrave churchyard. Tradition says he is the figure holding the whip, while his brother Charles holds the horse's halter. Gypsy funerals can be elaborate affairs, when many families bring extravagant floral tributes, and expensive memorials

are erected. The *Suffolk Chronicle* of 12 April 1851 says John Chilcot's funeral was exceptionally well attended. Several later relations of the Chilcots were buried here, including his cousin Repronia Lee. An obituary notice in the *Bury Post* of 18 March 1862 (calling her 'Lepronia') says that her female relations held a wake where they spent the night in 'moaning and lamentations' which were 'dreadful in the extreme'. (James John Hissey's *A Tour in a Phaeton Through the Eastern Counties* (1889) records a belief that Repronia Lee was the queen of the gypsies, but this was probably an exaggerated local tradition inspired by the romance of a gypsy grave.)

Thomas Brinkley was the water bailiff of Ipswich from 1861 until 1872. His gravestone in Ipswich Old Cemetery (plot R) stands on the east side of the main footpath between the Belvedere Road entrance and the cemetery chapels. A water bailiff is a law enforcement officer who polices an area of water to see that it is used properly, and prevent misuse, obstruction or unauthorised fishing. The 1871 census records Thomas Brinkley living at 9 Foundation Street in Ipswich, with his wife Eliza. Born in Ipswich, he was then aged 61. I can find little about him in the *Ipswich Journal*, but on 10 July 1869 he is reported as being responsible for the Ipswich Oyster Fishery. The carving suggests that Thomas Brinkley was also an engineer, involved with dock maintenance.

William Jacobs's headstone, also in Ipswich Old Cemetery (plot E) shows that he was a policeman. The 1881 census, supplemented by a brief death notice in the *Ipswich Journal* of 5 January 1884, records that he was born in Coddenham in 1832, and lived at 11 Withipool Street in Ipswich with his wife Emily and three children.

William Cooke's gravestone, showing an interesting scene of blacksmith's tools, under God's 'all seeing eye' forms part of a row of graves running alongside the pathway through the north side of St. Margaret's churchyard at Lowestoft. The 1881 census records William Cooke as a blacksmith, living at 10 Gun Lane, with his wife, four sons, two of whom were blacksmiths, two daughters, and a 16 year old 'blacksmith's lad' who boarded in the house.

A railway locomotive appears on John Nicklin's headstone in Lowestoft cemetery in Normanston Drive (plot 5, grave 220). An engine driver for the Great Eastern Railway Company, he died in 1887, aged 64. The 1881 census showed him as resident at 224 North Raglan Street in Lowestoft, with his wife, Caroline, and his 17 year old son, also called John, an engine fitter. He gave his place of birth as Liverpool. He would therefore have been six at the time of the Rainhill Trials, when the first practical railway locomotives were demonstrated at Liverpool, and seven when the Liverpool-Manchester

Railway, the world's first passenger railway, opened. He thus lived through the era when the railways revolutionised life in Britain, and transformed Lowestoft from a declining harbour town into a national holiday resort and an international fishing port.

George Frederick Cotman's gravestone in the churchyard of St. Peter and St. Paul's church in Felixstowe shows that he was an artist. Born in Ipswich (a collateral descendant of John Sell Cotman), he was a society painter, specialising in social and domestic genre scenes.

Ufford church is well known for its spectacular font cover. One Sunday morning in September 2006 I discovered another unusual treasure in the churchyard. I saw that there would be a pet's service at Ufford. Thinking this would be an enjoyable event, I went along, to find that it was being held outdoors. During a lull in the service I looked around the churchyard and saw some unusual marks on this memorial: at the first opportunity I ran over to see what they might be, and discovered that it was a gardener's gravestone: the inscription was badly worn, but I could just about make out the date 1814. After the service I mentioned my discovery. Amazingly, nobody had previously been aware of this, and the churchwarden showed the details to the people at the service, including the children and their pets: one of the high points of my church visiting career.

'The Boy's Grave' stands on the B1506, on the county boundary, at a crossroad between Newmarket, Kentford, Moulton and the Cambridgeshire village of Chippenham (national grid reference TL687661). The *Bury Post* of 11 April 1876 reports a court case when a gamekeeper described how he followed poachers to the 'Boy's Grave' at Moulton. I was told the story of the grave by my grandmother, Mrs Margaret Halliday (nee Starling) who was born in the nearby Cambridgeshire village of Ashley in 1878 and lived until 1976. She said that a shepherd boy thought he had lost a sheep. Afraid of being blamed for its theft, and hanged or transported to Australia, he hanged himself. He had miscounted: no sheep were missing. He was buried at the crossroads, since when gypsies have cared for his grave in secret. A belief has developed that the boy was a gypsy. In the 1980's a story began to circulate that a local squire liked gypsies and let them camp on his lands. When the squire employed a young gypsy as a shepherd resentful house dwellers stole a sheep and let the gypsies take the blame: the squire drove the gypsies away and the boy hanged himself in shame. This does not correspond with traditional gypsy life: while excellent horsemen, gypsies do not keep sheep. On 15 August 1985 *The Newmarket Journal* revealed that a woman from Northolt in Middlesex was making fortnightly trips to look after it. Noel Aves from Moulton has recently assumed the task after being told that visitors on Jockey Club tours of the area were disappointed to see it neglected.

Dobbs' Grave stands on the west side of a road bend in Dobbs Lane in Kesgrave (national grid reference TM238456). A Dobbs family appears in Kesgrave parish registers between 1721 and 1740, but nothing is known for certain about the eponymous Dobbs. A local folktale says that villagers, celebrating the completion of the harvest in the Bell Inn at Kesgrave, wondered if there was a body in the grave. Going to excavate they found a human skeleton: one of the group took a tooth from the skull and kept it as a charm on his watchchain. 'Dobbs Corner' appeared on the 1805 Ordnance Survey map of the Colchester and Ipswich area, when a second, lost, track formed a crossroad here. By the end of the nineteenth century there was a belief that 'Dobbs' was a shepherd; local tradition now holds that he was a gypsy who may have been hanged for sheep theft. Early in the twentieth century a concrete headstone and footstone were placed over the grave; in about 2000 it was enclosed by a metal fence. Recently a hedge has screened 'Dobbs' Grave' from the road, but it can still be found without too much difficulty.

The custom of burying suicides by a crossroad was abolished by Act of Parliament in 1823. It may have derived from the belief that the burial at a crossroad would confuse the suicide's ghost and prevent it from returning to haunt its home. At the Boy's Grave and Dobbs' Grave, the unfortunate person buried there has received sympathy and consideration that they may not have known in their lives, thus being re-admitted to the community. Folklore may associate gypsies and shepherds with roadside graves as gypsies frequently camp on marginal land, often near crossroads, while shepherds lead a lonely existence in remote fields.

There is an 'outcast cemetery' at Onehouse (national grid reference TM033592) attached to the nearby 'House of Industry' (or 'Workhouse') for Stow Hundred, which opened in 1781. Workhouse inmates were denied some of the normal dignities that might reasonably have been accorded to members of society, including a decent funeral: their bodies were wrapped in a sheet and deposited in the workhouse cemetery in a shallow grave that was normally filled with quicklime to speed decomposition. Graves were marked with wooden crosses, displaying a metal number rather than a name. Eventually it was decided that even this was too extravagant, and numbers were simply painted on the crosses. The last burial took place here in 1933. Stow Union is now used for residential purposes. In 2008 Onehouse

parish council opened the site as a public amenity and nature reserve called 'The Pauper's Graves'. Some pauper gravestones survive; the numbers from some other graves were attached to a modern cross which was blessed by the parish clergyman, so those buried here finally received something approaching proper respect and consideration. Although 'The Pauper's Graves' is somewhat difficult to find, access only being by a footpath across the fields, it is now a surprisingly pleasant location.

A small Jewish community formed in Ipswich in the eighteenth century: it acquired a synagogue in Rope Walk in 1791 and a cemetery in Fore Street in 1796. The community dispersed and the synagogue was demolished in 1877, but the cemetery remains in a business car park near the junction of Fore Street and Star Lane. Surrounded by a brick wall, it is not open to the public, but it can be viewed through the metal grill that serves as a gateway. It contains 35 head and footstones with Hebrew inscriptions, dated between 1804 and 1850. A small plaque on the right hand wall marks the boundary between St. Helen's and St. Clement's parishes: was there a conscious choice to site the burial ground at the boundary of two parishes?

Headstones in Ipswich Jewish cemetery.

The Society of Friends (or 'Quakers' as they are popularly known) were often keen to establish their own burial grounds. There is an attractive Quaker cemetery in Turn Lane in Woodbridge. (The adjoining Meeting House was built in 1678: it closed after the last regular attender died in 1931, and is now a private house, but its beautiful exterior can still be seen from Turn Lane.) In 1988 a scheme to build houses on the burial ground caused such an outcry that Woodbridge Town Council leased it on a peppercorn rent and opened it to the public. It is now an interpretation centre for Quaker history, a nature reserve, and a place for study, meditation and relaxation. Quakers disapproved of gravestones as a 'vain custom' and did not permit them until 1850, when they were to be of uniform design, and only show the deceased's name, age, and date of death (to be recorded as, for example, '19 of 2 month' since Quakers objected to the traditional names of days and months, such as Monday or January, because they were taken from pagan beliefs). Thus, while there were over 350 burials here between 1679 and 1937, there are only nineteen headstones, including that of the local Quaker poet, Bernard Barton, erected by some of his admirers.

Some churchyard memorials display distinct forms of religious observance. Russian Orthodox crosses in Claydon churchyard commemorate Sophie and Konstantin Benckendorff. Sophie, a daughter of the wealthy Russian Shuvalov family married Count Alexander Benckendorff, the Imperial Russian ambassador to Britain: their daughter Nathalie married Jasper Ridley, a younger son of the First

Viscount Ridley, they lived in Mockbeggars Hall in Claydon. Alexander Benckendorff died in office in London in 1917. Unable to return to Russia after the Revolution, Sophie moved to Limekiln House at Claydon. On her death in 1928 she was buried under a Russian Orthodox cross. Her son Konstantin made Claydon his home: he was buried beside her in 1959. (His autobiography, *Half a Life*, describes his early life in pre-revolutionary Russia; his wife, Maria, a distinguished harpist, was buried nearby.) There is a third wooden cross in the extension churchyard on the opposite side of the road.

The Garrett works at Leiston made some cast iron grave monuments. This memorial to Richard Garrett I's brother-in-law, Henry Newson, stands in Leiston churchyard. A monument to Francis Robinson, one of the last bailiffs of Dunwich, in St. James's churchyard in Dunwich, was obviously produced by the Garrett factory, as it is made to the same design as Richard Garrett II's memorial in Leiston churchyard.

In 1843 brothers-in-law David Ward and James Silver opened an iron foundry at Foundry House, on the west side of Long Melford High Street (next to the Cock and Bell Inn). By 1881 'Ward and Silver' employed over sixty people. The firm closed in 1953. James Silver was buried under a cast iron memorial, west of Long Melford church tower. Cast iron grave markers made by Ward and Silver can be seen in Long Melford churchyard, particularly to the northeast of the church.

Joseph Noller of Saxmundham died in 1727. His gravestone in Saxmundham churchyard contains morning and afternoon sundials in an oblong cavities on the east and west faces, marked 1, 2 3, 4, 5, so that the shadows fall through the recess (12 noon is omitted because the stone would then be in shadow). The dials point to the North Star, making them parallel with the earth's axis.

Joseph Forester's headstone, dated 1796, is reminder of one of the most poignant tales in the history of Suffolk: the decline and fall of Dunwich. In the thirteenth century Dunwich was as large as Bury St Edmunds and Ipswich, with six parish churches, but it was destroyed by coastal erosion. All Saints' Church was the last of the town's medieval churches to survive the encroachments of the sea. Eventually this fell into ruin because the shrunken community

was too poor to maintain it, but the churchyard continued to be used for burials until 1832, when the modern parish church of St. James was opened. The ruins of All Saints' Church and the surrounding churchyard have gradually been worn away by the action of the sea, but this gravestone remains on the edge of the cliff, a memory of the destruction of the once important seaport of Dunwich.

During the Napoleonic Wars a barracks was built in Woodbridge, which housed 5,000 soldiers (more than the town's civilian population at the time). After the Battle of Waterloo it was dismantled. Over ten years rather more than 800 soldiers stationed here died, and were buried in a cemetery to the west; this memorial, placed to record the location, is the last visible trace of the establishment. A municipal cemetery was later established on the site: this stone can best be seen from the public highway through the cemetery railings on Warren Hill Road, to the east of the cemetery gate.

In rural Suffolk (and elsewhere in England) there was a prejudice against burial on the north side of the church (this was not so common in towns, if just because more people were buried in churchyards). As churches are traditionally oriented east-west, the north side lay in shadow for most of the day. In Matthew 25:31-46 Jesus says that when he comes to judge the nations, he will call the righteous to his right and the damned to his left. (Popular expressions illustrate this bias: 'sinister' is the Latin word for 'left', while a 'right hand man' is a favoured person.) It is supposed that suicides, executed criminals, the unbaptized or excommunicate were buried on the north side of the church. Hadleigh parish registers record that this was applied in two cases of a criminal and a suicide in 1634. In the greater majority of churches featured in this book the main approach is from the south. Thus southern burials were clearly visible to those attending church, and it would seem as if these were included in the community. At Aldringham, Brent Eleigh and Great Saxham the main approach to the church is from the east, yet there are no early headstones on the north side of the church. The tradition is strikingly illustrated at Ingham, where the church stands in the centre of a churchyard facing the Bury-Thetford Road, so that it presents its west front to the village street. Yet while the southern half of Ingham churchyard is filled with memorials, the north side is virtually empty.

John Cullum, the sixth baronet of Hawstead, was also the rector of the parish. In 1770 he wrote a detailed *History and Antiquities of Hawstead*, in which he complained about his parishioners' aversion to burial on the north side of the church, leaving the south side of the churchyard was overused. He requested to be buried on the north side, hoping that his example might change popular preferences. His grave stands by the north door, between two medieval coffin lids. His stance had little effect, for there are still few gravestones on the north side of the church.

Some churchyard memorials are notable for their size, such as this statue of Anthony Wingfield, who died in 1714, at Stonham Aspal. It is the work of Francis Bird, the most prestigious sculptor in Britain at the time, whose entry in *The New Dictionary of National Biography* describes him as 'a sculptor of baroque verve'. The Wingfield family lived at Boughton Hall nearby; Nikolaus Pevsner's entry for Stonham Aspal in the *Suffolk* volume of his *Buildings Of England* series says 'the design is so unlike anything one is used to in churchyards that one feels a monument in Westminster Abbey may be taking a country holiday'. It is a remarkably fine representation of the costume of a wealthy man of the time: wearing an expansive cravat around his neck and an elaborate wig on his head, he reclines in Roman style: he originally held an asp in his raised hand, but this disintegrated due to exposure to the elements.

Henrietta Robins (nee Duncombe) who died in 1728, aged 42, has a monument on the south wall of Badley church. The Duncombe family lived in Battlesdon in Bedfordshire. Henrietta's sister, Isabella, had married Richard Gipps, the lord of the manor of Badley, and had been buried here ten years previously, which may be why she chose to be buried at Badley. The family coat of arms takes a prominent place, while the representations of a sarcophagus and an urn show a classical influence. This is larger than any of the interior monuments in the church: perhaps it was placed here as there was not enough room for it inside.

George Page, 'the Suffolk giant' was buried in the churchyard of his native parish of Newbourne. Growing to a height of 7 feet 4 inches (some accounts say 7 feet 7 inches), he and his brother, Meadows Page, who was 7 feet 3 inches tall, travelled the country with Whiting's circus as 'the Suffolk giants'. He died when he was only 26. (There is a brief obituary in the *Bury Post* of 10 May 1870.) The footstone at the end of his grave stands significantly further back than those of the adjoining graves, to accommodate his exceptionally long coffin. The headstone is now badly worn, but the epitaph read 'Sacred to the memory of George Page, the Suffolk Giant. Died 20th April 1870 aged 26 years. He was exhibited in most towns in England but his best exhibition was with his blessed redeemer.' His grave inspired John Owen, a novelist from Felixstowe, to write a novel about his imagined life with the title *The Giant of Oldbourne*.

Although many memorials have been cleared away from the eastern section of the churchyard of St. Margaret's church in Lowestoft, a few exceptionally tall headstones have been left in situ. By far the largest of their kind in Suffolk, it is unclear why they were so large, unless it was to ensure that they stood out in what was an unusually crowded churchyard. I stand 5 foot 10 ½ inches tall: to give an idea of their size I posed against one of them.

Caroline Murat's memorial at Ringsfield is made in a French style that reflects her ancestry as Napoleon Bonaparte's great niece. Her memoirs say that she was named after her grandmother, Caroline Bonaparte, Napoleon's youngest sister, who married Napoleon's cavalry commander, Joachim Murat. Their son, Lucien, moved to the U.S.A., where he married an American. Caroline Murat was Lucien's oldest daughter: she was born in Bordentown, New Jersey and brought up as an American, but her family returned to France when she was 16, after Napoleon III took power. Marrying Charles de Chassiron, a distinguished diplomat and art collector, she was a maid of honour at Napoleon III's wedding to the Empress Eugenie: when they mislaid the wedding ring she supplied one of her own rings in its place. With the collapse of Napoleon III's regime she came to England. When Charles de Chassiron died she married John Lewis Garden of Redisham Hall at Ringsfield. She expressed dislike of country life in Suffolk, preferring the company of high society in more fashionable places, but she was buried beside Ringsfield church in 1902.

William Bardwell's monument at Southwold is a strong candidate for the county's most elaborate churchyard memorial. Born in Southwold, William Bardwell wrote several architectural textbooks. He submitted a design for the new Houses of Parliament in 1835, a complicated pastiche of all previous English architectural styles, which is generally regarded as one of the more amusing and impractical plans. He collaborated with Rigby Wason, the M.P. for Ipswich in an extravagant scheme to redevelop Westminster (which never left the drawing board). His only major architectural commission was Glenstal Castle in County Limerick in Ireland, an elaborate neo-Norman structure. William Bardwell designed this memorial to himself and his family in Southwold churchyard: like many architects, he fantasised about redesigning his home town. He corresponded with the vicar on restoring the church (his plans were not accepted) and he drew up plans for a new town hall (which was never built). It is intriguing to think how Southwold might have developed had his talents been allowed free rein.

Thomas Mills, a wealthy merchant in Framlingham, was a Baptist at the end of the period when members of that faith could still suffer persecution for their beliefs. Living to see more enlightened attitudes prevail, on his death in 1703 he left money to establish an almshouse in Framlingham, to which residents could be accepted regardless of their religious affiliations. He directed that his body was to be laid to rest in a tombhouse in the grounds of the almshouse. He left his fortune and business interests in the care of a servant, William Mayhew, who was buried in the tombhouse with him ten years later. Thomas Mills asked that the residue of his estate should be used to fund the education of local children, leading to the establishment of the Thomas Mills School in the town. On the anniversary of his death in 2003, to uphold their founder's ideals, the school established 'The Thomas Mills Tercentenary Fund' to help educate children in Third World Countries. Thomas Mills may have asked to be buried in the grounds of his almshouse to ensure that people would be reminded of his legacy, or, as an act of defiance to the Church of England to show that he had evaded burial in the parish churchyard. The Mills Mausoleum stands beside Station Road in Framlingham. While there are several older mausoleums in Britain, these were attached to churches: this is the earliest example to have been built in private ground, away from a church.

This mausoleum in Hacheston churchyard was built for Chaloner Arcedeckne, an Irish aristocrat who made a fortune as a plantation owner in the West Indies. He returned to Britain to buy a country estate at Hacheston, where he had Glevering Hall built. Chaloner and three other members of the Arcedeckne family were laid to rest in the mausoleum between 1804 and 1812. The blank recessed arches and the shallow stone roof show classical influence.

After the Napoleonic Wars Edward Bliss, a London property speculator acquired a 2,500 acre estate at Brandon, on which he built Brandon Park. He had many trees planted in the area, possibly to create employment, as there was much poverty locally at the time. His family mausoleum, which was erected in Brandon Park in about 1836, is one of the first such structures to have been built in the Gothic Revival style, as well as an excellent example of the Breckland use of knapped flint in building construction. Edward Bliss was laid to rest here in 1845, followed by his wife, Sarah, fifteen years later. When another family acquired Brandon Park in the twentieth century the Bliss's remains

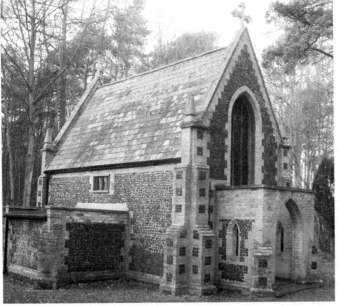

were removed to the parish churchyard. Edward Bliss's mansion is now a private nursing home, but Brandon Park is now an attractive public amenity and nature reserve, open to the public throughout the year. While the mausoleum (like most such structures) is normally locked, the exterior can be seen whenever Brandon Park is open. (People wishing to visit by car may be expected to pay a parking fee.)

Thomas Hallifax, a London banker, bought Chadacre Hall at Shimpling in 1823; this mausoleum for his family was built beside the parish church in 1850. It combines the influence of classical architecture in its solid stone walls and roof and the Gothic Revival in the pointed blank arches and door lintel.

In 1867 John Purcell Fitzgerald of Boulge Hall (Edward Fitzgerald's brother) commissioned the architect William Gillbee Habershon to rebuild Boulge Church. The contract included this family mausoleum in the churchyard. John was an uncompromising 'low church evangelical' Anglican, who seems to have been ready to propound his beliefs at any opportunity. Edward Fitzgerald held liberal religious views, and was not a regular churchgoer. This was a cause of contention between them, to the point that Edward asked to be buried outside the mausoleum. While largely in the same Gothic Revival style as Boulge church, the rectangular stone roof bears some resemblance to that of the *Mausoleum of Halicarnassus* (the Greek monument which gave its name to these structures). Personally, I think this is one of the most attractive examples of its kind anywhere in Britain.

# THE VICTORIAN ERA
# AND MODERN DEVELOPMENTS

In the Victorian era a growing desire to honour the departed permeated all levels of society: not only by erecting funerary monuments, but staging elaborate funerals and observing conspicuous mourning rituals. One striking development of this age was the development of the public cemetery. There was an overwhelming need for new burial grounds as an unprecedented rise in population automatically led to a rise in the death rates, while a growing concern for public health made it necessary to dispose of the dead in a hygienic and medically acceptable way. Nonconformists and Roman Catholics, too, were agitating for the right to bury their dead in accordance with their own religious beliefs, without being compelled to use Church of England burial grounds. These, and other pressures led to the passage of the Burial Act of 1855 which allowed local authorities to set up public cemeteries. Ipswich, Bury St. Edmunds and Framlingham were quick to take advantage of this; every town, and many villages soon followed suit. Classical concepts of aesthetics were employed, as cemeteries were landscaped with wide pathways and shady trees, a conscious echo of the classical gardens of Arcadia.

During this era the production of funerary monuments increased exponentially, fuelled by improvements in industry and technology which meant that good quality stone, slate, and even marble, could be quarried efficiently, transported by railway to all parts of the country, then carved into memorials with great ease and at lower costs than ever before. By the end of the nineteenth century professional monumental masons operated in every town. A trade postcard, issued by Frederick Herbert Goddard of Bury St. Edmunds, shows a display of ready-made stone and marble gravestones waiting to be inscribed with epitaphs. Between 1888 and 1929 F. H. Goddard is listed in *Kelly's Directory of Suffolk* as operating from King's Road, (which ran from the town centre to the municipal cemetery). A message on the back, to Harry Spalding, the sexton of Flempton, says that Mr. Goddard hopes to visit the churchyard to fix a marble curb on a new memorial. (I am grateful to Sue Rawles of the Bury St. Edmunds Postcard Club for lending me this item from her personal collection.)

Since I have insufficient space in which to describe every nuance of the Victorian monumental mason's art, I have chosen a few representative examples from the Old Cemetery in Belvedere Road in Ipswich to show some of the most popular designs. Pointed tops are common. These may have been influenced by the 'Gothic Revival', by far the most preferred style for church building, also employed in many cemetery chapels and cemetery lodges (as well as much civic architecture). As it would have been difficult to fit text into the space, the gaps at the top of the memorial were often infilled with floral patterns. This was aesthetically pleasing, while, as we have seen, flowers were perishable, and thus reminders of mortality. Victorian funerals were characterised by a development of floral tributes, a custom which remains popular to the present day.

Clasped hands were a popular design, representing a farewell to earthly existence and God's welcome into heaven. If the sleeves enclosing the hands were masculine and feminine they symbolised marriage.

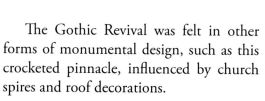

A bird could represent the soul leaving the body; its outline shape was suited to fill the pointed top of a headstone. It often carried a leaf in its beak to symbolise peace.

The Gothic Revival was felt in other forms of monumental design, such as this crocketed pinnacle, influenced by church spires and roof decorations.

Circular topped gravestones may have been influenced by Romanesque (or 'Norman') architecture, which was characterised by round arches. There was also the aesthetic consideration, that, while curved or pointed tops were more expensive to make than rectangular ones, they were more pleasing to the eye.

Classical motifs continued to exert an influence on funerary art. Urns remained popular, sometimes covered by drapery as a sign of mourning.

A broken column, partly inspired by classical ruins, symbolised a life cut short. This memorial honours two brothers who drowned in shipping accidents at the ages of 17 and 23.

Sometimes chest tombs were made from single blocks of marble.

After the Reformation the use of a cross as a religious symbol had been frowned upon by many Protestants as 'idolatrous' and 'popish', but over the nineteenth century cross-shaped churchyard memorials became popular (perhaps because pictures of the crucifixion appeared in illustrated Bibles).

Towards the end of the Victorian era reactions against what was seen as the mechanisation of society led to such artistic and social programmes as the *Arts and Crafts Movement,* which sought to reintroduce traditional craftsmanship, using simple forms and individual designs. This influenced many aspects of British art and architecture, including churchyard and cemetery art as its exponents began to commission their own memorials. Edwin Lutyens, one of the most important British architects to be inspired by this movement, was responsible for some of the simplest and most moving developments of modern funerary art, as the slaughter of the First World War led to the formation of the Commonwealth War Graves Commission. It would have been inappropriate to honour the deaths of so many brave young men with ostentatious sculptures. Instead Edwin Lutyens designed a standard headstone which allowed for a few brief particulars and images to be applied to all war dead. Nearly every churchyard and public cemetery contains some of these dignified reminders of their poignant sacrifice.

An enclosed area in Ipswich Old Cemetery contains eighty Commonwealth War Graves Commission memorials to eighty victims of the First World War, aged between 19 and 43.

The naval cemetery beside Shotley parish church is maintained by the Commonwealth War Graves Commission in honour of members of the Royal and Merchant Navies who have lost their lives on active service. Overlooking the Orwell Estuary, it probably commands the most spectacular panorama to be seen from any burial ground in Suffolk.

Twentieth century gravestone art has seen some reactions against standardisation of design and calligraphy. The impact of twentieth century artistic movements and 'functional' design, has led to a certain restraint against the wilder excesses of gravestone ornament.

For many centuries the Christian religion was generally opposed to cremation because of the belief in the bodily resurrection of the dead. But this was legalised in 1885. Modern population increase, concerns with hygiene and propriety, and technological advances have made cremation acceptable and now over 70% of the dead in Britain are cremated. The ashes can be scattered at a location chosen in advance by the deceased, or afterwards by relatives; if interred in a designated burial ground they can occupy a proportionately smaller memorial. A recent trend has been the environmentally and ecologically conscious 'green cemetery', where permanent monuments are abandoned in favour of trees or earth mounds that will merge into nature: in some ways a return to the anonymity of the medieval churchyard grave. Death is inevitable. The way people treat the remains of the dead shows their attitudes to this final rite of passage and the way they wish to remember past generations.

# Animal Graves

Some people have felt such gratitude to animals for their affection, company or service that they have decided to commemorate them with a permanent memorial. All the pet graves I know of in Suffolk are on private land, such as gardens, estates or parks. I have chosen to show examples that are reasonably accessible to the general public, but people wishing to see these are advised to contact the relevant property in advance to find out about admission times and charges.

A plaque on a wall in Euston Park, reads: 'Trouncer 1788 Foxes rejoice, here buried lies your foe'. Trouncer's master, Augustus Henry Fitzroy, the Third Duke of Grafton, was Prime Minister from 1768 to 1770, but left politics to devote himself to his estates. Trouncer was his favourite dog. Robert Bloomfield, 'the Suffolk poet', was born in 1766 at Honington, on the Grafton estates. His best known poem, *The Farmer's Boy*, mentions Trouncer's grave, and praises Trouncer with such lines as:

> Pride of thy race! With worth far less than thine
> Full many human leaders daily shine!
> .. Nor flowers are strewn around Ambition's car:
> An honest dog's a nobler theme by far.

Robert Bloomfield often expressed compassion to animals, and disliked animal cruelty.

Two nearby stones record Garland, 'the spotless rival of her grandsire's fame'; and Duchess, 'a faithful and singularly intelligent spaniel … killed by an accidental shot while performing her duty in the Decoy Carr'. The three plaques are at about eye level on a wall to the west of the track from Euston village to Euston parish church.

This dog's cemetery is a small fragment of Hardwick House, once the home of the Cullum family. It was made by George Milner-Gibson-Cullum, the last of the line. Touching inscriptions, dating from 1894 onwards, name 'poor old Dandie', 'Jeanie, mother of many children', 'Horace West, beloved of Thusie' and 'poor blind Peter', who drowned in 1918. A memorial to 'Ching', a retriever, bears the badge of the Second Life Guards, and names his owner as 'Fen. Inst. (fencing instructor?) W. Elliott'. While Hardwick House was demolished after George Milner-Gibson-Cullum's death in 1921, the surrounding park was left as a public amenity on the edge of Bury St Edmunds. The West Suffolk Hospital was built over part of this in the 1970's, but modern development missed this plot. The cemetery is not well known: concealed by undergrowth to the northwest of the staff car park, it may be difficult to find. While there are no restrictions on visiting it, those going to see it should be ready to either expect a long walk around the hospital grounds, or pay hospital car park fees.

Thornham Hall at Thornham Magna was the home of the Henniker-Major family. Major General Arthur Henry Henniker-Major, a younger son of the fourth Lord Henniker, served with the Coldstream Guards in the Egyptian campaign of 1882 and the Boer War. Arthur's wife, Florence, was a literary friend of Thomas Hardy. Arthur and Florence set up an animal's cemetery at Thornham Hall, where Arthur honoured his horses, 'Bob', 'Joll', 'Punch' and 'Toto' with monuments describing their military careers: Suffolk's only memorial to the many horses who have served in wars and military actions. Some of the Henniker-Major family's later pets have been buried here (including a black Alsatian with the ominous name 'Dracula'). Thornham Hall burnt down in 1954, but the park was rescued from dilapidation by the eighth Lord Henniker who decided to admit the public: now known as 'Thornham Walks' it is a highly enjoyable attraction, open to the public all year round. (Admission is free, but people wishing to visit by car may be expected to pay a parking fee.)

Lanwades Hall at Kentford, an amazing example of neo-Jacobean architecture, was built by James Larnach with his winnings after his horse, Jeddah, won the 1898 Derby. Later owners set up memorials to six dogs southwest of the Hall. These include 'Dinah, the best of retrievers', 'Bert most beloved of dogs', and 'Volo' whose headstone displays the often repeated statement 'the more I see of man the more I love my dog'. Lanwades Hall is now the headquarters of the Animal Health Trust, a leading centre for veterinary research: among other important projects, it operates a breeding programme for the Suffolk Punch. Parts of the grounds are open to the public at certain times, when the dog's memorials can be seen. Unfortunately Jeddah's memorial is on private land and inaccessible to the public, although there are hopes that this might one day be returned to public view.

Little Hall in the Market Place at Lavenham was the home of twin brothers John and Thomas Gayer-Anderson. They laid out a very attractive garden, which contains memorials to Peter, an Aberdeen terrier, and Zoobzie, a Siamese cat. Thomas Gayer

Anderson's delightfully personal guide to Little Hall says that 'Zoobzie' means 'gay lord', and says she was 'the most delightful and beloved pet we ever had'.

Helmingham Hall has been the Tollemache family's home since the fifteenth century: Alexandra (Xa) Tollemache, a leading garden designer, has created an exceptionally beautiful garden which is open to the public on certain occasions during the summer months. It contains sixteen wooden memorials to the family's dogs, dating between 1960 and 2006. The latest, to Jester, bears the Latin 'semper felix, semper fidelis': 'always happy, always faithful'.

The National Stud at Newmarket includes a quiet and dignified cemetery for champion racehorses. Nine distinguished horses have been honoured with burial here: normally the head, heart and hooves were interred under the memorial. (Unfortunately EU regulations have since prevented horse burials in this manner.) Never Say Die, the champion sire in 1962, was the first Derby winner to be ridden by Lester Piggott. Silver Patriarch won the St. Leger in 1997, while Tudor Melody was the leading two year old of his generation.

Mill Reef is the most famous horse to have received a special burial at the at the National Stud. The winner of the Derby in England and the Prix de L'Arc de Triumph in France in 1971, he is also honoured by a beautiful statue nearby. The National Stud maintains strict security, but visitors can see the racehorse cemetery as part of guided tours which take place daily between February and October. (Tours are very enjoyable, but may need to be pre-booked. It is advisable to contact the National Stud in advance to confirm ticket prices, times and availability.)

Remus, a Suffolk Punch, was a star attraction at the Museum of East Anglian Life in Stowmarket. Arriving in 1980, he was the museum's working horse, used for agricultural work, logging, and giving cart rides. He retired in 2000, but remained a popular visitor attraction. On his death seven years later, he was believed to be the world's oldest Suffolk Punch. He was cremated, when his ashes were interred at a specially convened ceremony, after which this memorial was erected over the burial site. Remus's grave can be seen whenever the whole museum area is open to the public.

An exquisite carving of a Suffolk Punch appears on John Lankester's headstone at Bawdsey. He was chief horseman to the Quilter family of Bawdsey Manor, breeders of Suffolk Punches.

A member of the Wyard family of Castle Farm at Offton was found dead in the stable with his horse standing guard over him. The scene has been recreated in a rather affecting sculpture on top of the family memorial in Offton churchyard.

A horse appears on Abraham Easter's headstone, on the northern edge of St. Mary's churchyard at Woodbridge. The 1841 census lists him as a farrier in Castle Street.

This splendid sculpture stands northeast of St. Margaret's church in Lowestoft. The inscription commemorated Samuel Gage who died in 1874, aged 19. The *Ipswich Journal* of 28 March 1874 says he was the son of William Gage, a fly and omnibus proprietor. He wanted to ride, but his father wanted him to help at a funeral. In anger Samuel drank some prussic acid. It is now impossible to know why he reacted in this way: maybe he only wanted to alarm his father or express his anger, and did not anticipate the results of his actions; maybe he had other problems or difficulties that we cannot now know about. But he evidently took great enjoyment from riding, and his family worked with horses, which might explain this choice of headstone.

Several headstones in the public cemetery in Normanston Drive in Lowestoft show a horse mourning over his master's (or mistress's) grave. This is possibly the best example, on Samuel Boardley's headstone (plot 13, grave 75). He died in 1900, aged 42: the 1881 census recorded him as a carter. Then aged 23, he was newly married to Mary, with a one year old daughter, living at '3 Boardley's Buildings'. His profession meant that he would have regularly

worked with horses. By the time of his death he had moved to Wilde's Cottage in Wilde's Score: the 1901 census suggests that his wife continued to run his business.

James Clark is honoured by this elaborate memorial in the public cemetery in Bridge Street Road in Lavenham. The 1891 census says he was a cab proprietor and owner of a livery stable at 70 High Street.

This gravestone at Monk Soham must be one of the most moving representations of military combat in the county. It honours Garson Ralph Chapman, who died in 1921 from wounds received in the First World War. I spoke to Garson's niece at Monk Soham: she said he was riding his horse in battle when a bomb exploded near him and he fell into a shell hole. Is the angel receiving his soul or protecting him?

# EPITAPHS

Epitaphs can poignant, or even amusing. It might be interesting to conclude with some epitaphs which I have found in Suffolk.

Quakers often created their own burial grounds (see *Unconventional Graves*). When such a plot in Quakers Way, Leiston ceased to be used a stone was placed there, with an inscription on one side:

> In the year 1670 this piece of land was purchased by the Society of people called Quakers and for many years used as a burying ground for their dead, in 1786 it was planted with trees and this stone placed.

This poem was on the other side:

> Mortal! Look here, think on thy own frail state;
> And learn from this, thy only most certain fate.
> Here, mixed with dust, obscure from mortal's eye,
> The mouldering bones of ancient worthies lie.
> This grave is raised for that sufficient end,
> To guard their dust, and mouldering bones defend,
> And this is raised, their monumental stone,
> Not to record their deeds, but say they are gone.

The cemetery now forms part of the gardens of two private houses, and is not accessible to the public.

A gravestone in Acton churchyard commemorates Mary Sanderson mistress of the dairy to George III's wife, Queen Charlotte. Her will, in the Public Record Office, says that while she lived in the London parish of St. Martin's in the Fields, she wished for her body be taken to Acton for burial (this is mentioned against her burial request in the parish registers, although neither source explains why). The document goes into great lengths about the distribution of numerous gowns, petticoats and stockings to relatives, and refers to £200 consolidated funds in the Bank of England. The epitaph, the lower part of which has been worn away, reads:

*Sacred to the Memory of*
MRS MARY SANDERSON
Late of the Queen's House in London
and Mistress of Her Majesty's Dairy
*Who departed this life 8th Feby 1783*
*Aged 38 Years.*
This stone was erected by her disconsolate
Friends, as a small token of the respect they
owe to so Amiable a Woman.
In love she liv'd; in Friendship died:
Her Life was ask'd, but God denied.
*We boast no Virtues, nor beg we any Tears,*
*Yet Reader, if thou hast but Eyes and Ears,*
*It is enough Oh! Tell me why*
Thou com'st to gaze? Is it to pry?
Into our loss? Or borrow?
A copy of our sorrow?
Or dost thou come
To learn to Die?
Knowing not whom
To practice by?
If this be thy desire
The draw thee one step nigher
Earth n'eer showed nor heaven a fairer.
She was but room denies to tell thee what,
Sum all perfection up and she was that.

At Somerton Charles Mills had his memorial made during his lifetime. A large chest tomb, the epitaph reads:

> This little sepulchre was made
> In which to have our bodies laid,
> The bodies of myself and wife
> When we are destitute of life.
> Because 'tis made before we're dead,
> And her in good health appear,
> I understand some have said
> That I'm eccentric, strange and queer.
> Indeed!
> Why Jacob, in Genesis, we read,
> Did dig his grave before he died,
> And Joseph of Arimathea beside
> His tomb hath hewn, St. Matthew saith
> Out of the rock before his death.
> Now, two such precedents as these
> May give those troubled at it – ease!

There are tales of conscious (or unconscious) humour in epitaphs, such as the memorial inscription which says 'erected in memory of John Smith, who was drowned in the river, by his wife'. These are usually apocryphal. I read about a headstone to a woman called Lettice Manning at Moulton, displaying the couplet:

> Oh cruel death to please thy palate
> Cut down Lettice to make a sallet.

I was inclined to dismiss this as another such story, but I decided to search Moulton churchyard for it. It is indeed on a headstone, quite close to the south wall of the church. Unfortunately it was rather worn, but just about legible: she died on 11th July 1737, aged 49.

There is another amusing story about Thomas Gardner, the Southwold antiquarian, whose *Historical Account of Dunwich* remains an essential sourcebook for local historians. His first wife and daughter pre-deceased him and were buried in Southwold churchyard under a headstone whose epitaph began:

> *Virtue crowned, during life*
> *Both the daughter and the wife.*

He then married a widow, who also died before him. Her headstone started:

> *Honour ever did attend*
> *Her just dealings to the end.*

In 1769 Thomas Gardner was buried between the two headstones, prompting the epitaph:

> *Between honour and virtue here doth lie*
> *The remains of old antiquity.*

As Thomas Gardner's gravestone was becoming badly worn it was moved inside the south aisle at Southwold church in honour of his services as a historian, which has saved it from further deterioration, but rather spoils the epitaph's deliberately intended humour.

Another headstone, near the south gate of Southwold churchyard, commemorates David May, a sailor killed by pirates in the Caribbean while serving on the West Indiaman

*Ann.* His burial does not appear in the parish registers (he was probably buried in the West Indies) but his widow still wished to honour him with a gravestone in his home town. The epitaph reads:

> *Nor yet have ceased to flow a widow's tears*
> *O'er scenes remember'd most the lapse of years,*
> *On foreign seas he fell, but not by storm*
> *Which boisterous winds the heaving tides deform,*
> *Nor by the rock beneath the tide concealed,*
> *Nor by the sword which warring nations wield,*
> *But by the foe received in friendship's guise,*
> *By hands of treacherous pirates lo he dies.*
> *Thou too art mortal, hast'ning to thy grave,*
> *Believe on him who ever lives to save.*

Close by a small headstone to Charles May bears an appropriate epitaph for a member of a maritime community:

> His anchor was the holy word,
> His rudder blooming hope,
> The love of God his maintos'l [main topsail]
> And faith his sailing rope.

A tragic accident was reported in The *Bury Post* of 17 August 1785:

> Yesterday afternoon we had the most dreadful and violent storm of rain and thunder ever remembered in this town. A fireball fell on Crown Street which killed a little girl, slightly hurt her mother and did considerable damage to the house in which they dwelt.

Mary Hasleton, the girl who died, was only nine years old, and saying her prayers at the time. Her family were Roman Catholics. There is a large memorial to her on the Charnel House in the Great Churchyard in Bury St. Edmunds. The tragedy may have prompted the question of how God could let such a thing happen, for the verses:

> Not Siloam's ruinous tower the victims slew
> Because above the many sinned the few;
> Nor here the fated lightning wreak'd its rage,
> By vengeance sent for crimes matur'd by age,
> For while the Thunder's awful voice was heard
> The little suppliant with its hands upreared
> Addressed her God in prayers the Priest had taught
> His mercy crav'd and his protection sought.
> Learn reader hence, that wisdom to adore,
> Thou cans't ner scan & fear his boundless Power:
> Safe shalt thou be if thou perform'st his will,
> Blest if he spares and more blest should he kill.

The Tower of Siloam was a building in Jerusalem, which collapsed, killing eighteen people. In Luke 13:4, when Jesus was asked if those who died unexpectedly were being punished for their sins, he cited this to show that a sudden and unexpected death could come to anybody, regardless of how good or bad their previous life may have been.

Sometimes a short, succinct comment can be revealing. A plaque erected in memory of Mary Dorling, on the north wall of St. Mary's church in Bury St Edmunds, simply says:

*Say what a wife should be and she was that.*

Epitaphs to people of exceptional longevity can be of interest. A nearby plaque on the same church reads:

*In memory of Orson Bidwell and Sarah his wife. He died 4th March 1768 aged 90 years. She died 18th Nov 1779 in the 102nd year of her life.*

To the north of Stowlangtoft church I found the headstone of Catherine Major, who died in 1842, which displayed this poem:

*The churchyard grass is fresh and green,*
*Small wild flowers on each grave are seen,*
*And all around most truly saith*
*Theres nothing terrible in death,*
*If only thou thyself who die'st*
*Does live and die in Jesus Christ.*

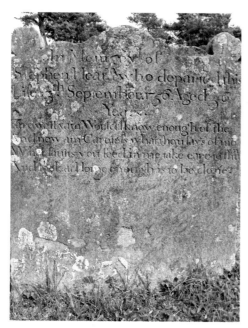

There is a touch of cynicism at Sutton:

*Farewell vain World, I know enough of thee,*
*And now am careless what thou say'st of me,*
*What faults you seed in me take care to shun*
*And look at home enough to be done.*

At Kersey there is the disparaging comment:

*Reader pass by nor waste thy time,*
*On bad biography or bitter rhyme,*
*For what I am this humble dust enclose,*
*And what I was is no affair of yours.*

The Affleck family of Dalham Hall placed memorials to their servants on the outside wall of Dalham church. One, which modern readers might regard somewhat ambivalently, pays tribute to two estate workers:

> Near this place lies the body of John Keates labourer of this parish who died 17 Nov 1820 aged 89.

> Also the body of Joseph Brett labourer of this parish who died 30 Jan 1822 aged 75.

> Each of these worthy men served the family of Dalham Hall honestly and faithfully with little interruption for half a century.

> Who change their places often change with loss,
> 'Tis not the rolling stone that gathers moss.

At Hacheston there is a tribute to John Mann, an estate steward at Glevering Hall:

*Pope boldy says some think the maxim odd,*
*That an honest man's the noblest work of God,*
*If Pope's assertion be from error clear,*
*One of the noblest works of God lies here.*

(The Pope referred to was the eighteenth century poet, Alexander Pope.)

Another headstone at Hacheston records a common sentiment:

*Short was my time*
*The longer my rest,*
*God called me hence*
*Because he thought best,*
*Therefore dear friends*
*Lament for me no more,*
*I am not lost*
*But gone before.*

The Worlingworth Local History Group has produced an excellent pamphlet, *Monumental Inscriptions of St. Mary's Church, Worlingworth*. The maxims they record include one of the most commonplace epitaphs to be found across Suffolk (I have also seen this at Barking and Little Whelnetham):

*Afflictions long I bore,*
*Physicians were in vain*
*Till God did please*
*And ease me of my pain.*

John Chenery, who died in 1817, is commemorated by a message echoing similar sentiments:

*I was with sorrow sore oppress'd*
*Which wore my strength away,*
*Which made me wish for heaven's rest*
*Which never will decay.*

The headstone of John Jessop, a bell ringer, who died in 1825, bears the lines:

*To ringing from his youth he always took delight*
*Now his bell has rung and his soul has took its flight*
*We hope to join the choir of heavenly singing*
*That far excels the harmony of ringing.*

Lydia Pettit's headstone, dated 1838, has the couplet:

*Beneath this earthly silent sod*
*Lies one who firmly trusted in her God.*

Cleo Creasey, dated 1891 contains the inscription:

*The harvest is the end of the world*
*And the reapers are the angels.*

A brief aphorism appears on William Weavers's headstone of 1841:

*Praises on tombs are titles vainly spent*
*A man's good life is his best monument.*

Possibly the most thought provoking epitaph I have seen is that of John Wink in St. Mary's churchyard at Bungay. While I have been unable to find out anything about John Wink, it seemed a highly appropriate ending to this book:

Look, Think, Reflect, Repent,
Be assur'd theres nothing
So certain as Death.
He can only be truly happy
Who lives today
As if he were to die tomorrow.

# INDEX OF PLACES
# MENTIONED IN THE BOOK

## REFERENCES ARE TO PARISH CHURCHES
## UNLESS OTHERWISE SPECIFIED

Lightning Source UK Ltd.
Milton Keynes UK
UKOW01f1538070114

224095UK00001B/14/P

9 781845 495954